CW00523633

Pamela grew up in Yorkshire, moving to the Home Counties with parents in her teens. Until her early twenties, she worked in London department stores and as a nurse at St. George's hospital.

After spending several years as a stay-at-home mum, Pamela studied for a degree in English at Reading University, followed by working in technical and non-technical editing posts for some years. More recently, she taught ballroom and Latin American dancing in partnership with her husband John, for local authorities and independently. This came to an end in 2008, when John was diagnosed with Parkinson's disease.

To Dorothy & Neil,

With Love,

Pamela

For my beloved husband, John
27th May 1933 to 16th November 2016
In my heart forever

The story tells it all.

Pamela Ratsey

THE TALE OF A HIP

AUSTIN MACAULEY PUBLISHERS™

LONDON • CAMBRIDGE • NEW YORK • SHARJAH

Copyright © Pamela Ratsey (2018)

The right of Pamela Ratsey to be identified as author of this work has been asserted by her in accordance with section 77 and 78 of the Copyright, Designs and Patents Act 1988.

All rights reserved. No part of this publication may be reproduced, stored in a retrieval system, or transmitted in any form or by any means, electronic, mechanical, photocopying, recording, or otherwise, without the prior permission of the publishers.

Any person who commits any unauthorised act in relation to this publication may be liable to criminal prosecution and civil claims for damages.

A CIP catalogue record for this title is available from the British Library.

ISBN 9781788788380 (Paperback)
ISBN 9781788788397 (Hardback)
ISBN 9781788788403 (E-Book)

www.austinmacauley.com

First Published (2018)
Austin Macauley Publishers Ltd™
25 Canada Square
Canary Wharf
London
E14 5LQ

With grateful thanks to Dr. Desmond T. Pim (D.C., D.O., N.D., M.N.I.M.H.), my long-term chiropractor and mentor, for helping me not to give up when challenged by fate.

My thanks also to our Strictly-style dance teachers for their patience and expertise, to our many dance pupils and to those who so positively supported the experimental exercise classes.

January 2017
Romance

A few days before the New Year I wept in plain sight, in a busy restaurant buzzing with people out to enjoy. Not a few discreet tears dabbed hastily away then forgotten, body and soul immersion in the isolated misery of loss.

Cheery entities had been jabbering incessantly around me from the moment I got into the car, to be driven between silent fields slipping darkly past beneath a crisp winter's sky, to a place I did not know and could not see.

Glancing neither to right nor left I got up from the table and headed out to the garden, where the frost covered grass gleamed softly beneath festoons of white lights adding seasonal sparkle to the perimeter fence. I stood rooted to the spot, detached and empty, impervious to the cold.

A few weeks earlier, after three days without opening his eyes or speaking a word, John had garnered the remnants of his rapidly dwindling resources to call Pam, for the very last time.

I let my lips lightly touch his tired eyelids and stroked his cheeks gently with the backs of my fingers, then supported his delicate pale hands reassuringly in my own. The faint smile fleetingly animating the spent muscles of his face gave me strength.

"You can let go now," I said with no hint of tremor, calmly resigned. Within seconds he did.

In the space of a breath the air in the room stood still, and both of us were free. Torn between grief and relief, every cell in my body shook with ferocious intent, casting the shattered remains of the one half of a duo I was only moments before into the healing winds of eternity.

***

The heady days of our courtship, spent mostly within easy driving distance of our parental homes, were almost as exciting as foreign travel, still a rarity in the fifties, as indeed were cars. I have always loved London, days by the sea, and spectacular sunsets.

I was a student nurse at St. George's teaching hospital at the time, based at Hyde Park Corner for body work and Wimbledon for the brain, with occasional study blocks at Tooting.

John had just returned from National Service in Ceylon, in his case deferred for a few years due to the official status of his employment, from which at the customary age of eighteen he could not be spared.

Back from seeing the world, lean and brown, and attractively matured, he came to see me straight off the plane, eager to find out where he stood with respect to my hopefully waiting heart. It was his before he went away.

Free tickets for the musical show 'Salad Days' and the classic western 'Gunfight at the O.K. Corral' added extra excitement to the already spine-tingling experience of living in a budding global super-hub. When I visited with my parents a few years earlier, Heathrow was two runways and a wind-sock.

With a solitaire beauty soon sparkling on my third left finger life grew even sweeter, and hopes for the future were high. Walking hand in hand beside the Thames, kissing lovingly beneath the stars, dancing the old-fashioned way, eating new-fashioned burgers and Italian ice-cream, the world was a magical place.

No sex before the big day of course. At the slightest suspicion of a giveaway bump Dad would have gone mental, and Mum would have hidden her face in shame. On reflection it could have ruined everything, including this story. The pill had not yet been invented.

Gloria was my only rival. John absolutely adored her.

I loved our leathery old banger too, except when she staggered to a petulant halt half way up a hill in a part of the country civilisation had not yet reached, and sat there complacently smoking refusing to budge.

Under-bonnet skills were essential for a car owner before the advent of the microchip. With perseverance and elbow grease, John usually managed to coax her back into action without needing to call an expert.

Every now and then though Gloria would blow a gasket and play dead, sometimes requiring a long hike to the nearest telephone kiosk.

On our way home from the west country in the twilight, we ended up spending the night at a farmhouse in the middle of nowhere, with a promise from the petrol station with one pump and a ramshackle workshop that our eccentric friend would be fit and raring to go by ten o'clock the next morning.

I could have sworn the garage mechanics winked at one another as they helped me down from the open truck bidding us goodnight, but by then it was too dark to be sure.

I stared for a moment at the spotless double bed, took a deep breath, and asked the farmer if there was a second room as we were not yet married. I even showed him 'the ring' on the naïve assumption that he would be suitably impressed.

"Very nice," he said, turning away with barely a glance. "Do you want bacon and eggs in the morning?"

I nodded, feeling suddenly like a naughty child deprived for no good reason of its comfort blanket.

"Hard luck," the farmer mouthed in John's direction, as the two men left the room.

We spent our honeymoon in a small hotel on the rive gauche, a stone's throw from the Sorbonne – as much frothy coffee as you liked plus as many croissants as you could eat, and a pay as you go meter on the bath (bring your own plug, and ask for the key).

We ate as many as politeness would allow. Finding something affordable and preferably recognisable for lunch was a daily challenge.

From about six-thirty in the evening, a tramp with a bowler hat and bright red kerchief claimed his bed for the night, by sitting on the ventilation grill above the hotel's basement kitchen. This shocked me at first, and made John wary, but the poor chap seemed good natured enough, and to his credit not even a tiny bit sorry for himself.

If he was not too far gone, or had not yet fully downed his bedtime quota, he removed the hat with a theatrical flourish, setting it carefully on the grill beside him before wishing us bonne nuit, then pulled a ragged coat over hat and head and curled up in an anonymous heap. He and his empty bottle were always gone by morning.

A charming Frenchman tried to pick me up on the steps of the Musée d'Orsay on our very first day, suggesting lunch at a fashionable restaurant. He was very smartly dressed, and could almost certainly afford it.

Seeing John approaching with gruyère filled baguettes and fizzy drink, I pretended not to understand and showed him my left hand, at which point he vanished like a shadow in the rain.

Each evening as we sat down for our meal a camel took a measured stroll past the hotel window, apparently quite alone. As we were finishing off the wine it did the same thing again, in the opposite direction. No-one so much as shrugged a shoulder. Vive la France!

My first trip abroad bore no resemblance to the indulgent luxuries apparently essential to honeymooners of today. Our room was spacious and clean but quite basic, with a cracked wash basin complete with dripping tap, a much-used armchair, and curtains that looked as if they had been there since the Revolution. The daily shared platter plus carafe ordinaire lacked even the most innocent of the fifty murky shades.

But none of this mattered. We were together, in Paris, after London the next best place to heaven.

My business as usual hormones, with no sense of timing and profound disrespect for occasion, kept us in limbo for the best part of a week, while we climbed the Eiffel Tower, roamed in a romantic haze among the artists in Montmartre, and visited Notre Dame, where to my dismay a funeral was in progress.

The guided tour continued regardless, but I doubt I heard a word. From time to time a whiff of incense drifted across my nostrils, making me feel sick. My eyes kept returning in macabre fascination to the ceremony at the heart of the vast medieval space, closing down someone's life step by chilling step as it had through the ages.

When the all-important 'it' finally happened it was over in seconds, in too much haste on John's part and with little or no involvement by me. It was disappointing to say the least. I fell pregnant within weeks, wondering what all the fuss was about.

Although a little more time to adjust might have been nice, we were happy enough about the baby. As inveterate idealists we had consciously decided to leave the initial schedule to nature, but struggled to come to terms with our dashed expectations of how the act of creation really should be.

Talking about it was not an option. The three letter pestilence now shameful and shameless on every front page was then utterly taboo in respectable society. Neither of us would have known where to begin.

In the swinging sixties, when sex came out of the shadows in a blaze of uninhibited glory never again to be denied, and the maharishi was preaching love and peace to all with flowers in his hair, we found ourselves marooned in a bubble of semi-detached ignorance, drowning in a sea of emotions we had no words to express.

My mother thought sex was a God-given healer for marital ills. When she was finally brave enough to let me in on this unsuspected secret, I saw my frail petite mum in a totally new light, as a knowledgeable woman of the world who could potentially help me navigate the mysteries of my unknown and unknowing depths.

But with supreme indifference her all loving Maker robbed me too soon of the only person I could possibly have confided in on so sensitive a matter. After seeing her only child wed, and sending out slices of cake, Mum held her baby grandson twice, bought him a toy drum for his first birthday, then was gone.

In our case sex itself was the ill. We wanted, how we wanted, true and perfect connection, but it was always denied.

Just once I felt stirrings and started to moan. In a glimmer of burgeoning ecstasy I hovered expectantly on the brink, preparing to be swept away on an enveloping wave of sublime emotion, but John thought he was hurting me and stopped. It never happened in quite that way ever again.

My forlorn hapless lover would sometimes clam up for days, shutting himself away from the merest hint of conflict inside a tightly sealed shell. When in due course he emerged from his latest bout of not so splendid isolation he was his sunny attentive self once more, until the next time.

I sometimes blamed sometimes pitied myself, but there was nothing either of us could do about it. The culprit was misaligned bones, John's as well as my own. It was a very long time before we found out.

Counselling by a stranger, as likely as not to be divorced or what used to be called living in sin, would almost certainly have driven us apart. Love and silence somehow kept us as one.

Clueless as many of us were at the time about the most fundamental human experience the full joy of sex continued to elude us, but over time we learned to take pleasure from physical closeness without the full Monty.

In today's know it all world, exposed to all things erotic from the cradle, I would probably binge shop at Ann Summers, and fake it like crazy.

***

Two years ago we moved away from Reading, where we had lived for several decades in two houses, to a bungalow at the heart of England a short driving distance from our daughter. John looked for the stairs every day when we first arrived, and got lost trying to find the kitchen for quite a long time.

After only four months in our new home things still felt strange to me too, even lying in bed.

"I don't want to wake up. This is not my birthday."

A moment of silence lulled me into a false sense of security, but the peace was short lived.

"I don't want to wake up. This is not my birthday."

I had spent the last fifteen minutes trying to ram home this simple fact. If I could stay motionless for long enough, we might both catch a little more sleep.

My upper body tissues were shifting uneasily again, stopping short of full commitment like a shiver that never quite shivers, and my left calf was building steadily to an overextended stretch. Remembering how painful this had been so often in the past, the mini reprise was almost a pleasure.

"I want to get up."

John said this most days, at four, five, or if I was very lucky six, with belligerence that riled me slightly although I knew he couldn't help it. As I could rarely persuade him into bed before midnight, sleep was in short supply for both of us.

He needed me to get up before he could, able to keep my own balance while assisting his, plus a wheeled walking frame with reliable brakes and a whole lot of patience.

"I don't want to wake up. This is not my birthday."

The first time he said it I came very close to tears.

With daylight tiptoeing half apologetically around the room it was probably about four thirty.

***

It seems only yesterday we were dancing for a very smart gathering at a very smart club in Henley-on-Thames, invited to entertain their local and continental guests by one of our private couples James and Sarah.

Considering my wayward bones and John's tricky back, they were taking quite a chance on our ability to deliver. John was seventy at the time.

To my relief there was no trace of the panicky shakes that had ruined so many things in the past. My hips for once behaved exactly as they should, letting my body and limbs flow freely as never before, or as things turned out ever since.

John too relaxed happily into the magic of harmonious movement, as for the first and only time we danced truly as one, through a romantic waltz, tantalising tango, and sexy rumba.

As soon as the music stopped an excitable Dane ran onto the floor and swept me off my feet, carrying me all the way round the room to rapturous applause that seemed never to stop. They gave us flowers and champagne.

The vicar thought he and his wife might like to join one of our classes. James and Sarah talked us up all the time.

When general dancing began, we wandered hand in hand through wide open doors into summer-warm air, to walk on manicured lawns sloping gently towards the river.

It was a star-crowned night at the end of May, one to remember.

***

February 2017
Yorkshire

Having lived my entire adult life in metropolitan commuter land, with easy access to town and country and national and global connections, at the age of eighty I now find myself alone in the middle of nowhere, with few contacts and no car.

The busy teaching schedule that had governed our lives for more than two decades began stuttering to a halt about ten years ago, when John started having mild seizures on Saturday evenings after demolishing the ritual spag bol with red.

In recent months he had taken to lying on the floor after the meal to ease his back, waiting for me to join him, or if the music and wine had done their job well enough to dance barefoot on the carpet scantily clad.

When it became apparent that he was likely to drift into a kooky dimension the moment his head touched the floor I took to kneeling beside him fully dressed, poised to react.

I would talk softly into his semi-conscious la la land to let him know I was there, adding that although his food as usual was great I could not vouch for the ice-cream and coffee.

He tried to reply with slightly amused lips, but the words were not clear. After a while he would suddenly open his eyes, sit up, and say hello, totally unaware that anything unusual had happened.

So sure was he nothing was wrong that he refused to see a doctor for months. When eventually he did, he was diagnosed with Parkinson's disease.

We taught ballroom, Latin American, and during the craze years a refined version of line dancing several times a week, in school and village halls in Berkshire and Oxfordshire, but by the time the fateful sentence was passed only a handful of pupils still remained. Many had grown old, or left the district, or simply moved on to other things. Soldiering on regardless would have benefited no-one.

Due to beginning the grieving process when I first opened our door to social care at the end of last May, with this year's spring now on its way I feel the worst is already behind me. Although trigger sights sounds and thoughts will doubtless continue to spill a tear for some time to come, my bleak heart and nerve-ridden abdominals are edging their way daily towards a new kind of normality.

The bungalow does not feel empty, because in a sense it is not. Undying love lingers protectively within its walls, shielding me as it always has from the big bad world, refusing to give up on the dream.

John's spectacles perched on a carved wooden nose on the dining room window ledge make me smile every morning as I draw back the curtains. In the evening, if the heartache returns, I wrap myself in his voluminous dressing gown, cradling the comfort ball clutched by his fragile dying fingers in reverently cupped hands.

I sit in the conservatory, where he lay silent in his willow-woven casket, walk on the grass where he took his final faltering steps, and feel safe.

'You can't let everything fall apart now, not after you have come so far.'

Star readings are still my daily tipple, despite never delivering more than a quick come hither snapshot of the possible road ahead before snatching it away.

'This time you will not disappoint.'

At this the sceptic in me leaps instantly to the fore. I have disappointed many times, mostly myself.

John came home with a pretty little writing desk one day, bought for three pounds ten shillings in a local junk shop. I treasure it still.

Money was scarce at the time, there were young mouths to feed, and unrelieved domesticity was beginning to get me down.

"You might like to try writing," he suggested casually, "a magazine article perhaps, or a short story?"

As I was currently in the process of applying for an evening job at the Post Office, with barely concealed anticipation, I suspect distraction was his most pressing aim.

***

When I was born the Second World War was mainly talk between government officials in secret locations. Less than two years on it was reality in every sitting room and pub, on every street.

Reality hardly touched me at all. My childhood was filled with art and music, stories at bedtime, and lots of loving care.

There was rationing of course, and the blackout, no sweets or bananas, and very few toys. But spring still came back every year with daffodils and April showers, and in the summer we sat outside the kitchen door shelling peas, picked only minutes before from the vegetable plot behind The Studio, where my father created beautiful things, and taught people how to paint.

Evacuees from London, with long a's and a small bag of personal belongings, came bewildered but hopeful to the relatively safe haven of the Yorkshire hills, where the lucky remained unruffled at home.

For the second time in living memory men walked away from their loved ones to serve king and country, filled this time with unspoken dread. History was not reassuring. Beneath the banner of fair play and freedom some became heroes. Many never came back.

My father never went. St. Vitus' dance in childhood had left him with an unstable nervous system unfit for active service, so he was sent to do his bit in a munitions factory instead. After collapsing into the machinery on day one, he was deemed to be a danger not only to himself, but also potentially to his fellow workers. His fighting days were over and done before lunch.

The Studio started out life as a chicken shed, and on the hot sunny day it was dumped in sections on our back lawn it smelt like it.

Uncle Pete came round to help. So to everyone's surprise did Jimmy and Paul, the terrible twins from next door, who mostly spent their time chasing one another round their garden kicking a ball that often landed in ours, arguing and scrapping loudly enough for the whole street to hear.

Their young Labrador Goldie came too, to stop her barking at them agitatedly from the other side of the fence. After saying hello to everyone with an excitedly wagging tail she settled down in the shade, keeping watch with half closed eyes.

Armed with several buckets of soapy water and a selection of scrubbing brushes the boys turned out to be pretty handy, and neither of them pulled my hair even once. They went home tired and happy, damp and dirty, clasping a sixpence each in one hand and a slice of freshly baked bread in the other.

The war did not entirely pass us by. Mum would sometimes wake me around midnight without switching on the light, and bundle me quickly into warm clothes and wellington boots.

Then the three of us would head outside towards the grassy hump between the potatoes and carrots, where a hand belonging to a voice I thought I knew would draw me from the moonless night into even deeper blackness.

"Come on in, dear. There's room 'ere for a little one."

We would squeeze in between shivering bodies on narrow wooden benches, gas masks at the ready, waiting for daylight or oblivion.

After the shelter door was slammed shut no-one said a word. When our teeth stopped chattering, and we began to sweat with closeness and fear, we each bit firmly on a chunk of hard rubber to prevent them from falling out. Goldie rested her chin on my knee, whimpering softly at intervals.

As long as engines were running, you knew you were fine. It was silence we dreaded, the heart-stopping void out of which a bomb might drop at any moment.

When the stomach-churning whirring finally faded into the night, en route perhaps for Liverpool or Bradford, torches were switched on, and everybody began talking at once, including our canine companion. We cheered at the top of our voices when a blaring horn sounded the all clear, then went happily back to our beds.

Whenever his leave was up Uncle Pete called round to say goodbye, looking wholesome and handsome in khaki. He would place his strong arms firmly under mine, and swing me round three times with my feet sticking out.

Then he brushed his lips lightly across my forehead, his neatly clipped moustache tickling my skin rather agreeably, before setting off to the bus stop at a pace, whistling 'Keep the Home Fires Burning' slightly out of tune.

It all seemed quite fun at the time, in retrospect rather romantic. Only when we learned he would never be coming again did I realise it was not. Uncle Pete was not my real uncle, but I loved him a lot.

At a time when everyone yearned for colour and light creative pursuits flourished. Dad's concert party 'The Hurricanes' was an overnight hit, as apparently was I. At the age of three I was booked for the guest spot in a Saturday night variety show in Halifax, equivalent to big-time in our then strongly parochial world.

At the sound of my name I had to walk out from the wings with my head held high, wave to the audience, and blow a kiss. Below the stage to my right, Daddy was settling himself at the piano. People whose faces I could not see were clapping. Many of them were wearing uniform.

A gaudy two-dimensional rooster, sitting on a pâpier-maché nest with stuck-on clumps of straw, had been set a safe distance back from the very bright, very hot footlights that I knew not to look at or touch.

My lip started to tremble as if I was going to cry, but it stopped immediately with the first note of the introduction to 'Hey Little Hen'.

With every 'when when when' I wagged a scolding finger, nodding my head vigorously at the same time, causing the tubes of hair lovingly coerced to perfection with strips of rag the night before to swing about energetically.

When I came to the 'Get into your nest do your little best' bit I moved my head from side to side, first quickly then slowly, like an exasperated wife chastising a lazy husband.

As I plunged both hands deep into the nest and pulled out two giant knitted eggs, lifting them high above my head to a splurge of closing chords on the piano, and a triumphant cry of "Cock-a-doodle-doo!" from the pianist, the laughter was thrilling.

If anything the response to 'The King is still in London', performed standing to attention in a scarlet-lined black cloak and gold painted crown, was even more enthusiastic. I saluted once, bowed twice, and marched into the wings, with hurrahs and bravos for me and his majesty filling every corner of the hall.

They gave me a glass of lemonade, and a wind-up clockwork horse. Then we went home, by taxi.

On VE Day everybody was up very early, hanging Union Jacks out of windows and bunting between lamp-posts, getting children into fancy dress, and sewing on ribbons ready for the carnival queen's parade, due to arrive at Farmer Dyson's field mid-morning for the judging.

There were bonfire parties, and dancing in the streets, and firework displays late at night. The air was filled with music light and laughter, and everyone was happy for a day.

We went to Whiteley's once for lunch on my parents' wedding anniversary, where we ate plaice and chips and Charlotte Russe, and sat on red velvet chairs.

Soon after we arrived a bouquet of white roses, pink carnations, and a mass of wispy greenery was delivered to our table, by a fresh-faced young waiter with a switch-on-switch-off smile, and clip-on-fall-off bow tie. Mum loved the flowers and the chips, but her cough was still a nuisance, even in summer.

A train was getting up steam a short distance beyond the side window, transporting me between mouthfuls to my favourite place on earth.

The capital was where Mr. Churchill lived and the king, the home of Peter Pan and the Old Curiosity Shop, and the household cavalry gleaming their way down Constitution Hill to The Mall, in scarlet tunics now we were at peace.

The next day it was liver and onion soup for lunch and cheese and jam sandwiches for tea. I never could make out whether we were comfortably off, or somewhere near the breadline.

* * *

Our nineteen thirty's house on the edge of the Chilterns had narrow steep stairs, multi-level gardens, and slopes every which way. It had served us well for more than thirty years, but no longer. Difficult decisions had to be made, preferably soon.

John had been trying to get me to take my clothes off all day, as had happened yesterday and the previous Tuesday. Whenever an opportunity arose he clamped me in arms of steel that threatened to displace my ribs for the second time in my life. I had never been afraid of him before in sixty years.

My ribcage was dislocated when the sternum was pushed forward during the birth of our first child, but I only realised this twenty years later in my forties. By then a sideways glance in the mirror was showing body distortions in every direction.

"Sometimes I think I've got six days, sometimes six weeks."

John was rambling again, looking pitifully lost.

Social advisers assured me I could revert to being a proper wife if I put him into a care home, but this did not ring true. Having his hand held for an hour or two a day, and the occasional 'there there' from a neat and tidy visitor bearing gifts was not what he wanted.

The vice-like grip suddenly released, as he latched on to fragments drifting aimlessly in his mind.

"This will be the last night of my life."

The doom-laden proclamation came like a bolt from the blue, startlingly insistent.

Quite suddenly I wanted to laugh. Melodrama was absolutely not his style. He sounded like a ham actor practising his lines.

The bond forged through struggle and mutual support over most of a lifetime would be rendered null and void in an instant if I handed him over to strangers.

"Open a bottle of wine."

Plonk Blanc was all we had in, about right for scrambled eggs and brown sauce, screw-top fortunately, I never did get the hang of corks.

"I don't care if I never see a hill again," John said wearily, as I poured him a glass.

The thought seared my soul, but I could live without if I had to. My tears that time were for both of us.

He had recently fallen out of bed twice in as many weeks, needing paramedics to rescue and patch him up on both occasions. One day I found him standing with his zimmer frame at the top of the stairs, poised to come down.

In the starkness of that life-defining moment only one person really mattered.

As soon as was practical we left the hills behind.

***

March 2017
Imagination

I recently moved back into the room that was ours, became John's, remained empty for a while, and now is mine for keeps.

From the bed we used to share I see what he saw almost to the exclusion of all else for the final months of his life, including conservatory windows, the bird box under the eaves, and trees of varying shades of green in our secluded rear garden.

The impulse to scurry indoors and turn the key after a short walk to the corner shop is thankfully a thing of the past. I now initiate as well as reply to good mornings, and where it would seem churlish not to on occasion say hello to a dog.

I spent twenty minutes on the stairs in Debenhams the other day walking down up down at each landing, to exercise hip and back muscles at angles not much used since our move to single storey living. Passers-by gave me clearance, pretending not to notice.

A shopper I suspected might not be quite what she seemed assured me I was not the 'elderly woman acting strangely' being discussed on her mobile. The ability to tell a white lie is probably written into a store detective's job description.

The topic of shifting bones seems to be one of the last taboos in our say-it-all bare-it-all society. Although medical specialists must have been aware of the phenomenon for centuries the rest of us are supposed not to notice, and get funny looks if we are foolish enough to say we have.

I have been blessed, or should that be cursed, with experience that has forced me to notice. Displaced joints have adversely affected my health in many ways, from headaches and fainting fits beginning in the teen years, to back and hip problems starting in my forties.

I used to think astrological predictions were rubbish. Now I'm not so sure. 'It's time to tell your truth' they advise me today, as usual slightly late. The star-savvy robot is already on her way.

During holidays down south as a child I used to sleep on three dining chairs propped against my cousin's bed. The middle one frequently slipped out of line, leaving me dangling in a droopy sling that sometimes bumped me to the floor.

Something in my lower back probably slipped too, although there are other suspects in the saga of my wandering bones.

At this time last year, with daffodils in bloom and early tulips getting ready to make their annual glory splash, we were just about coping, eating meals together at the kitchen table pretty much as we had since moving in. After breakfast John would fall into a strange kind of half sleep in his wheelchair.

When he came round about two hours later he would go looking for his walking sticks, eager to explore every corner of our new home while even the smallest glimmer of hope lingered.

Sometimes I would sit at the piano, and play the introduction to one of the love songs he had been singing for as long as I can remember. One of his favourites was 'Silent Worship' by Handel, 'Did you not hear my lady, Go down the garden singing?'

The sound of his vibrant tenor voice still sends shivers down my spine. I looked out the music today. Its pages are tattered and torn. Only now do I realise just how much he loved me.

Inside my head he is as beautiful today as he was in the sixties, singing his heart out to the left of the organ on stage at the Albert Hall, in black and white on the box. The massed choir was conducted by Sir Malcolm Sargeant. Our small children were tucked up in bed.

Only now do I realise just how much I loved him.

We were becoming more at ease in our new home by the day, although in the second spring since moving in John would still sometimes ask about the stairs, and got stuck regularly in a tricky corner of the lounge, or half way down the garden.

"It's nice here, isn't it," he said more than once.

"Yes it is," I agreed.

After forty years in electrical engineering he could still draw a fair representation of a square and circle freehand, but despite teaching dancing routines based on angles for twenty years the geometry of movement mechanics had deserted him completely. When he got stuck on the spot it could take a very long time to persuade his feet to turn through ninety degrees to get him moving again.

John's joints, like mine, had been under strain for most of his life. The congenital fault in his upper back had probably been causing quiet mischief from the day he was born. When seventy-five years later Parkinson's set in, and dopamine production failed, every bone in his body lost its way.

We talked about planting up hanging baskets and growing tomatoes again in our new greenhouse, as we had been doing for more than thirty years.

We drank cappuccinos outside the village café watching the world go by (twice) and went to see the hills that were there all the time if you knew where to look once (plus wheelchair of course).

We sat with our arms around each other every evening, pretending to watch the telly.

In a cocoon of suspended reality we waited.

***

I was born two months early at a nursing home in Huddersfield, where I spent my first few weeks of life in an incubator. A seven month baby was considered high risk back then.

The ubiquitous 'they' thought I arrived prematurely due to Mum's dad taking leave of the world just a few weeks before. Dust from the small slate quarry left to him by a relative he never met had transported him sooner than expected to that illusory 'better place' most people at least paid lip service to at the time.

In the not too distant past some people even believed in fairies. Photographs of them were distributed nationally, cavorting gaily at the bottom of someone's garden, with diaphanous wings and a secretive smile. Such deception took weeks of guile and dedication. The camera lens never lies, does it?

Now we can spread truths and untruths, tittle tattle and trivia to all corners of the earth in less than a second, over and over with no effort at all, via vacuous tweets and vain selfies. Are we wilfully scattering our souls with each click? The American Indians would certainly have thought so.

As a child I used to stay for a couple of nights once or twice a year at Grandma's house on the far side of town, in the room that used to be my mother's.

Robins, chaffinches, blue tits and sparrows tumbled in neatly ordered rows from picture rail to floor, repeated over and over on the pale blue background of the wallpaper. From the midst of sweet-smelling apple blossom, a few feet away from the open window, a blackbird's melodic notes danced joyfully on the morning air.

The front parlour was pure Dickens minus the cobwebs. Every knick-knack on the mantel-shelf was precisely placed. Between decorative boxes, china flowers, and ornaments of every size and shape, gleaming wood always shone. On a sunny day the curtains were partly drawn, to limit fading.

I would sneak in there sometimes to drown myself in the chills and thrills of its eerily suffocating atmosphere, saturated in the silently hovering dews of waiting mortality.

When darkness veiled my soul, as at some point it usually did, I would climb onto an arm of the huge velvet sofa, gripping it tightly between my thighs, to gallop on a magnificent steed with a white flowing mane to a brightly shining castle in the sky.

Then I would play 'Someday my Prince Will Come' on the tinny piano, and thump out a quick burst of 'Chopsticks' before heading off for tea.

Against the back wall of the parlour stood the table where a coffin once waited, since polished diligently every week. At its centre was a glass dome preserving two pairs of white gloves, a blue garter, a faded spray of silk flowers, and a sepia photograph of the just married couple in an ornate silver frame.

Neither of them looked particularly happy. Tying the knot was a serious business back then. The two candles standing guard in polished wooden holders had never been lit, but the hymn book nearby was still used most Sundays.

Granddad was carried a short distance along the road from there to his final resting place behind the Baptist chapel, within sight of the little wooden hut where he once filled out work sheets, paid his men, and made tea for passing ramblers, on a small fire set on slate among the grass.

If it was cold or damp cows would huddle nearby grazing and staring, then wander quietly away. The hut and kettle are gone now, but the cows still graze, still stare.

Grandma wanted to be a teacher, but like most girls of her social class ended up in the local woollen mill. Marriage to a man of moderate means was fortune indeed.

In her younger days she was a member of the Liberal party, delivering pamphlets and propaganda with glee. Even in old age the memory made her glow.

The highlight of her political career was the party conference at Scarborough, where she gave a rallying speech about what women needed to do next, danced in a different coloured dress each evening, explored the town in high heels, and dipped her toes in chilly waves before breakfast.

When the party was over she returned without complaint to the drab drapes of dreary domesticity.

'In olden days a glimpse of stocking was looked on as something shocking' Cole Porter reminds us. Now, wisely or not, absolutely anything goes.

"Your Gran were a reet feisty lass," so the neighbours would tell me admiringly, shaking their heads with ill-disguised envy.

Her bathroom was a wonder to behold, all glistening mahogany and brass, with acres of space. I spent a lot of time in front of the thrown up sash window looking out over the Pennines, letting the wind play havoc with the pale gold ringlets that were my mother's pride and joy, and my secret hate.

Mum was fun when she was well, but too often she was poorly. She taught me to read before I started school, and how to write the alphabet, in capital letters and small. She taught me to stand up for myself too, with partial success.

Before the NHS came to the rescue measles, scarlet fever and influenza, not to mention Mum's perennial chest problems, must have put considerable strain on the erratic income of a self-employed artist. Until the age of nine I was in and out of bed and school like a yo-yo.

Even with a raging temperature I knew when Doctor Mitchell was in the house. He took the stairs two at a time with ease, energising the air he moved through with purposeful vitality. His very presence made me feel safe.

When I was beginning to get better he would pluck a pack of playing cards out of thin air and show me his latest magic trick, or blow up the balloon he always seemed to have in a top pocket, rubbing it a few times on his lapel before releasing it to stick on the ceiling.

After he left I would ponder the mysteries of illusion and science for quite some time. Then I would read, from 'What Katie Did' to 'Alice in Wonderland', sometimes for hours, or make up stories in my head about my imagined older brother.

One wintry January, when Mum and I were struck down at the same time, the doctor came to see us two or three times a day, and sometimes in the night. The house buzzed from early to late with comings and goings, cold compresses and second opinions, kaolin poultices and clean linen.

When the fever was at its height, a nurse with squeaky shoes would pick me up off the floor, tuck the sheet in more tightly, and wash my face with cool water. Frozen peas were not yet an option.

Sotto voce discussions were held about the purplish black line on my arm, and when a bed might be available at the municipal infirmary. There was something wrong with my blood, and everyone seemed anxious. In the room next door pleurisy was developing into pneumonia.

In a state of delirium I looked out over an endless sea of people, all talking about me. Faces I thought I knew came forward one at a time or in groups to stare with intrusive half smiles, receding instantly if I stretched out a hand.

Just once I noticed Uncle Pete standing head and shoulders above the rest, very smart still in his fine soldier's uniform. When I pushed through the crowd to try and reach him he vanished.

As soon as I was allowed to go outside I stamped ugly brown holes in the pristine whiteness of the snow-painted garden, wishing almost at once that I had not.

**

April 2017
Life and Art

Yesterday morning, in glorious spring sunshine, I walked on grassy pathways bordering fields of young barley, towards the private airfield not quite visible from the back of the bungalow. In good weather planes taking off from there appear to skim the garden fence with a gleaming under-belly, before flying off into the blue.

The swathes of sparkling green guiding me across and between the runways were inviting. New-born energy and fresh air on my face sent a shimmer of joy through my long ailing heart.

Very briefly I caught a glimpse of a new-fashioned me waving a nostalgic goodbye to a world sadly gone, moving forward with confidence and optimism to shake hands with the future.

But the vision of new horizons quickly faded. Three quarters of the way towards my morning destination brambles and a large muddy puddle stopped me uncomfortably in my tracks.

My shoes were not right for the job, and I could not afford to lose my footing. Trying to stand up with nothing to lean on would be a gamble at best, and there was no-one in sight. Panic hit the pit of my stomach, and I decided to turn back.

Unable to escape the inner demons of uncertainty and fear I had hoped were gone for good I tried to run for the first time in ages, but uneven ground that had added interest during the outward journey now seemed loaded with treacherous intent.

The security fences robbing me of choice as they dictated every right angle turn became captors not saviours. Slowed by increasingly heavy legs and shallow breathing I felt terribly alone.

Today has been dull, damp, cold, and I have not been out at all. As dusk begins to fall, the orange-red strip of sky between the top of the fence and the canopy of our hundred year old apple tree reboots hope.

***

Hidden truths can shape lives in extraordinary ways.

Although my bones were on the move from quite an early age no-one noticed. Not even my father, who thought I was perfect in every way until I started to think.

Somewhere along the way I realised that despite, or possibly because of shining progress at school, I was probably something of a disappointment to him. My ability to draw was abysmal, and neither of us knew how to handle the transition from child to adult.

Dad was brought up in 'Last of the Summer Wine' country just outside Huddersfield, wild and beautiful, homely and plain speaking, church on Sundays. He was virtually born with a pencil in his hand.

At the age of fourteen, like siblings before him, he was sent to work in the mill, but unlike them found a way to escape, by becoming a window dresser at a smart shop in town.

His boss quickly recognised an unusual talent, and gave his new protégé time off to attend classes at the local technical college.

In the course of time the budding young artist passed teacher training exams with flying colours. His two certificates hung in pride of place on our dining-room wall.

As Dad's student days were drawing to a close an exotic aroma once tempted him into the Kardomah café, where he met the girl who had laughed earlier that morning at his attempts to attach a stray arm to a mannequin. Over freshly ground coffee and a plate of custard creams love's arrow struck, once and for a lifetime.

As always money in his parents' household was scarce, yet as if from nowhere funds became available for the dress suit he needed for the college graduation dance. Elated by her youngest child's success, and the prospect of a daughter-in-law with class, a proud mum will somehow find a way.

Other family members though were rather less pleased. Their baby brother was the cuckoo in their nest.

***

On a boring Sunday afternoon, when my parents were in the dining room listening to the wireless, I wandered out to The Studio, where I began rummaging idly through a heap of oil paintings stacked against a wall, wondering if the flimsily draped lady with sad eyes had been sold yet. I stared often into their brooding dark depths, as if seeking something I might have lost, or maybe had yet to find. I loved her long black hair. A panther-dark figure in the shadows was removing his trilby and an ornate leather belt.

Hearing Madge's voice, too close for comfort, I changed my mind and rushed out quickly to divert her. My personal pest had followed me home from Sunday school a few weeks ago, and ever since kept turning up on our doorstep with puppy dog eyes, looking as if she would like to lick me all over.

The only interesting thing about Madge was her two-wheeler fairy cycle with a rusty bell, and saddle-bag invariably crammed to the point of bursting. When I asked why, she replied mysteriously, "I might have to go away in a hurry."

As my legs were too long for the bike I used to whizz down the road with them stretched out forward, then lift my rear off the seat and pedal like mad to the top, to do the same again over and over. We were supposed to take turns. I fell off at least once a week.

One day the saddle-bag fell open, revealing a holey jumper, some pairs of rolled up knickers, a bedraggled teddy bear with one beady eye, and a beef dripping sandwich. I pretended not to notice.

"You're rich," Madge exclaimed excitedly, managing finally to wheedle her way into the house. "You never told me you were rich."

We lived in a three-bedroom semi with leaded lights on the front door and windows. There was a hand-hooked carpet and a poker-work coffee table in the lounge, and a mini Rodin's 'Thinker' sitting thinking on the hearth. In my world such things were normal.

The piano delivered by the rag and bone man by horse and cart on a very wet day, to a frenzy of twitching net curtains, had been tuned to within inches of its life, and stippled in two shades of cream to go with the décor.

"Can I see your room?" Madge asked, taking the scene in wide-eyed, and pawing eagerly at my arm. "I'd really love to see *your* room."

I put her off until next time, deciding there and then that there would be no next time.

Madge lived in a two up one down back to back with a junk filled yard, where the outside water closet leaked. The downstairs linoleum was faded and cracked, and the stairs were bare wood. Her mother answered the door in a dressing gown and curlers, even at mid-day.

"Mum's at it again with her latest," she said, as I prepared to dispatch her pronto. "He pushed me out and locked the door."

I edged her towards the kitchen, hoping to do the same, keen to spend the rest of the afternoon with my thoughts. 'It' was never mentioned in our house.

"I think he wants to kill me."

"Don't be so stupid," I shouted, feeling a sudden desire to slap her silly mooning face.

"I'd better go home then," she said, wiping away a tear.

I went up to my room, and stood staring for quite some time at 'The Return of Cupid', a water colour that had hung on my wall forever. The girl sitting near the bottom corner holding a red scarf was supposed to be me.

When the painting was put on display in the annual students' exhibition, the middle class ladies who flocked to Dad's art and crafts classes positively drooled over the three naked children with angel wings, poised among clouds amidst a fluttering of bluebirds. It was not for sale at any price.

"You should hold your own show in London, Professor, you really should," stated one of his super-gushers at the top of her voice. To my embarrassment and Dad's delight a small crowd gathered.

"We all think so, don't we?" the gusher added, clapping with gusto. Some people looked less sure than others, but everyone joined in.

With grammar school now on the horizon it was time to put away childish things. I had hardly ever played with the half dozen dolls sitting side by side against my bedroom wall, and packed them into a box for the orphans without a second thought.

I couldn't quite bring myself to part with Mrs. Rabbity though. The year I had bronchitis, and a cough that went on and on, she was sitting on top of a goodies-filled pillow case next to the bed when I opened my eyes on Christmas morning.

Her blue and white check pinafore was made out of one of Mum's old skirts from the make-do-and-mend box. Baby Rabbity was peeping out of the pocket. I loved them both to bits.

Tommy knew about 'it', I felt sure. He and I used to entertain audiences on the proscenium, while scene-changing was going on behind the curtains during Dad's travelling pantomimes.

From December to the end of February we performed at a different hall each weekend, once on Fridays, sometimes twice on Saturdays. Some people would turn up three times, even when the war was over.

I played the xylophone, Tommy the piano accordion, sometimes separately, sometimes together, sometimes classical, sometimes popular, ending with a Sousa march for tap-happy feet.

In addition to providing much needed light relief for a war weary nation, Dad liked to do a charity show proper from time to time. One year we took 'Cinderella' all the way to an orphanage near Sheffield in steadily falling snow.

The coach transporting the rest of the caste, plus family and friend helpers, got stuck part way up a hill, and everyone got out to push. The driver of our super-sized taxi kept going, in case we got stuck too.

After the show Mum took off her crinoline gown and star-spangled wig and went off to find a cup of tea. She loved playing the leading lady, but her energy often ran out.

Dad morphed quickly from Buttons to Santa Claus, and he and I handed out second-hand gifts to children with sallow skin and empty eyes, who treated me as if I was a visiting princess. I wished I could be a fairy godmother with a magic wand, and make their lives permanently better.

Wedged between scenery and props in the back seat of the car on the way home I couldn't stop thinking about Madge, who had vanished abruptly without saying goodbye. When I went to see if she was all right the windows of her house were boarded over, and the yard was ghostly still.

At the end of our very last performance Tommy presented me with my very first bouquet, and kissed me on the lips, in a way I quite liked but felt perhaps I should not.

The audience carried on clapping as if they had forgotten how to stop, so we played the closing march again, to the accompaniment of rhythmically stamping feet and raucous toy horns. I was ten, Tommy was thirteen. We were both dressed in sequinned white satin.

After the final Grand Finale a group of regulars who had been followers from the days of 'The Hurricanes' came up onto the stage with thank you cards and ginger beer, and the biggest cream sponge cake any of us had ever seen.

I loved my new school from day one. Every morning as I closed the gate in the back wall behind me I stepped into my own secret world. The garden was tranquil at that time of day, with butterflies sunning themselves on the lawn, perhaps a hedgehog or two in the border. Everyone else came in from the main road at the front.

A row of long skinny air raid shelters left behind from the war were hidden against the wall behind bushes, with a strident 'Out of Bounds' notice nearby. We went inside once for a dare, like girls did at boarding schools in old-fashioned stories.

***

I hated my boobs from the moment they began to appear, deeply resenting the unsolicited violation of the flat skinny self I had come to know and love.

Dad was not happy about the changes in me either. Solo trips to the park at the top of the road were suddenly a no-no. He wanted to know where I was every moment of every day. 'Beware of Men' was writ large across his forehead.

Whenever a bus turned up late and I arrived home five minutes outside his deadline he would rant and rave until Mum was in floods of tears, blaming me for her distress.

In year three I was allowed to get rid of the ribbon-tied bunches of ringlets and have my hair cut short – yippee!

The ferocious three-day headaches started at about the same time, and I fainted twice in one week, once in the kitchen at home, once on the music room stairs.

"It's her age," they said, "a mix of hormones and teenage angst. It will pass." As would often be the case in years to come, the worldly wise were only partly correct.

The move south part way through year four seemed like an exciting adventure until it actually happened. The maisonette was very small, with a narrow overgrown garden lit only by a solitary bright pink peony.

My daily piano practice must have driven the upstairs neighbours mad, but surprisingly they never complained. There was nowhere at all to set up an easel.

It was thought the warmer air of the Home Counties might help with Mum's cough, that it would be good for her to be near her sister, and my upcoming 'O' levels were unlikely to be much affected. A London base with galleries and the right sort of contacts had long been Dad's aim.

As things turned out the new way of life was quite disappointing. The curriculum and subject choices were different, and my Yorkshire accent might as well have been Chinese.

Mum's immaculately fashioned bright blue shirt and box-pleated navy blue gym slip did little to discourage turning heads, amidst a muted sea of stylish cream and brown. Cool I was not.

I stopped eating, or very nearly, and shrunk to six and a half stone, hoping to postpone indefinitely the advent of the despised nylon bra, with equally unwanted suspender belt and stockings.

As months passed by I looked more and more like a wraith walking, except for the stubborn roll of flab in the lower abdomen that heroically refused to budge, and is with me still.

Mum stood me in front of a mirror, not mincing words. "You are going down the drain," she stated bluntly. "Do you really think you look attractive like that?"

I pulled my stomach in as best I could then stayed perfectly still, blankly unresponsive, noting fondly the pale distant eyes, and concave contours of the alabaster cheeks. The ringlet-free look thrilled me to the core.

"Do you honestly believe a young man will look twice at a shadow? He would be afraid even to kiss your hand, for fear you might snap."

The funny thing was I'd always thought it was fat girls the male of the species did not look twice at. Not that I cared. At the time I was infatuated with the head girl at my new school, longing to run my fingers through her dark wavy hair, and hear a word for my ears only.

My newly whittled down waistline was doomed the moment the warmth of the oak-beamed café near Battle Abbey enticed us in. The smell of home-baked scones and bubbling plum jam negated my minimal food strategy on the spot. The visit to the historic site of the battle of Hastings had been interesting enough, but decidedly damp in dreary Sussex drizzle.

Due to their diminutive proportions the buttery little beauties were presented in half or whole dozens. Mum kept re-ordering until I was absolutely stuffed, looking happier than she had for a long time. As we were about to leave, she slipped a two shilling piece into the beaming waitress's pocket.

Standing outside the headmistress's study, hair combed, long a's at the ready and brown skirt carefully smoothed, I was not optimistic, but to my surprise I was received with a congratulatory smile.

My essay on 'The History of Mr. Polly' by H. G. Wells had been brought to her attention. She handed it over, marked nine out of ten 'Excellent', with a letter for my parents indicating that if at all possible I really should go to university.

I didn't even like the book, and was amazed by the reaction to my essay. Sixes and sevens G and VG had been more usual of late.

Dad had quickly discovered that the streets of London were not paved with gold and taken a job in an art shop, so I knew it was not going to happen.

A gauche newcomer with an aptitude for English but useless at cricket was unlikely to be put forward for a state bursary. There were girls in my class clever and mature enough to become doctors, and grants did not yet exist.

As it happened my appetite for books was in temporary decline, so the perceived deprivation was the equivalent of a second yippee.

Starting as a junior clerk in Personal Export at a department store in Kensington High Street, on the princely wage of three pounds fifteen shillings a week, I was off to paint the picture of my life.

***

On our first visit to the bungalow John and his wheelie friend had walked from the front door straight through to the back with scarcely a sideways glance.

After pausing at the conservatory step until someone came to help they had set off again, down the full length of the lawn to the greenhouse, at a pace not seen in months. We made an offer the very same day.

But our flurry of shared elation was short-lived. We had hoped to be able to walk to the corner shop together, perhaps even to the village green when confidence and capability improved.

It was not to be. Soon after moving in, John's muscle control began to deteriorate alarmingly. Yet again he had to be picked up from the floor.

Brushing the latest setback aside, he managed to convince himself that Parkinson's could somehow be stopped in its tracks by sheer force of will, and continued to fan the lone spark flickering amidst cooling embers for as long as he possibly could.

He had been hallucinating for some time, both before and after the house move, seeing spiders dropping from the ceiling onto our bed, someone outside the window peering in, and men sitting in *his* lounge, on *his* chairs, lusting after *his* wife.

"Why aren't you giving your gentleman friends a cup of coffee?" he used to ask, belligerently puzzled.

"There are only the two of us here dear," I would assure him gently.

"You were sitting on their knees earlier on," he insisted. "I saw you, first one then the other."

I would cuddle up close, taking comfort from his warmth. "Just you and me love, nobody else."

"It's nice here, isn't it?"

"Perfect."

***

41

May/June 2017
London

A skeleton in the process of returning to true alignment can sometimes have quite bizarre effects.

Shortly before we moved away from the Chilterns I found our local chemist closed one day. Supplies were needed for John, so having just missed a bus, and aiming to be away from the house for the shortest time possible, I set off down the hill towards the nearest alternative.

After the first few steps my feet started walking faster and faster on a mission of their own, ignoring entirely the common sense signals from my brain.

Attempts to rein in the muscles and set the rest of me back on track were fruitless, and I knew I was going to fall.

As momentum took over the pavement came up rapidly to meet me, and for a few blacked out moments of total oblivion I ceased to exist.

When I came round I was lying in the road, with traffic being diverted around me. A young woman who had just collected her daughter from school was mopping blood from my forehead and hands.

After a burly man from nearby roadworks had set me safely on my feet she took me to the doctor's surgery in her spotless new car, where I tried very hard not to drip. When the doctor had checked me over and the nurse had patched me up she took me home.

That evening, just as it was coming dark, there was a knock on the door. When I opened it nobody was there, but a bag containing the items needed for John had been left on the step, with a number to ring if I needed help. A car was purring discreetly up the hill.

***

For a sixteen year old ingénue from Yorkshire, typing labels for shipping and air lines, filling in exotic customer details with a biro in a big old-fashioned ledger, and a monthly excursion to the Bank of England to pick up customs documents was pretty exciting fare.

Add to that eating Mum's packed lunches overlooking the Round Pond in Kensington Gardens weather permitting, plus weekly singing lessons with an operatic coach in Bayswater, and a trip to the Oxford Street shops complete with newly opened pay packet on Thursdays, I was living the dream.

On my first day at work, Mr. Tootall (who was anything but) sent me on an important errand to an address half way up Kensington Church Street, armed with a sealed envelope explaining who I was, and the reason for my visit.

I listened intently to his meticulous instructions and low voiced injunctions to handle the parcel with care, then set off down the escalators from the fifth floor with my head held high, feeling really rather special.

Only when I arrived at the designated address did I discover I had been sent to collect Mr. Not-So-Tall's freshly laundered shirts. I ticked myself off for being so easily duped, determined not to be fooled again.

As I delivered the package with exaggerated care, I stared my pompous little mini-boss straight in the eye, with not the smallest flicker of a smile.

When neither of us was able to hold out any longer we both burst out laughing, and Mr. Tootall stood up to shake my hand. He was a pussycat really.

It was at John Barker's that I first fell in love, at least that's what I thought it was. Steve was the manager of the post room in the basement, always ready with a teasing remark and friendly smile. Trips from top to bottom and bottom to top of the store were required by one or other of us several times a day.

My heart skipped a beat every time a certain buff coloured overall crossed my eyeline. It was exactly like the one my father used to wear for working in The Studio.

One rainy afternoon Steve took me to the Odeon cinema at the end of the high street, on what nowadays would be called a first date. Then it was just going out. I was puzzled suddenly to be given half a day off, but thrilled by the invitation.

I don't remember what the film was, and doubt very much I would have cared. We held hands in the back row of the stalls, and from time to time a protective arm would wander casually around my shoulders, making me feel warm and happy inside. We ate popcorn with the trailers and ads.

The kiss placed on my lips with delicate fondness before accompanying me to the tube station to catch a train home told me as kindly as possible that it was all over. For one of us it never began.

Deep down I always knew Steve was too old for me, and not really my type, but the illusion was hard to let go. He looked so much like my long lost Uncle Pete.

I knew the city was a mistake within hours of my arrival. The culture did not suit me at all. The Victorian office block in a back street near St. Paul's was damp and old, the ambience spiky and cold. Employees scurried back and forth along narrow corridors and up and down gloomy iron staircases with barely a hello. To this day I have no idea what anyone actually did there.

I was presented with a list of meaningless numbers at the beginning of each working day, and introduced perfunctorily to a calculating device called Charlie, consisting of row upon row of metal levers that I did my best to get to grips with, but in truth never did.

The work was repetitive, and boring beyond belief. Left to get on with whatever I was supposed to be getting on with I did my best to be optimistic, but useful progress was never going to happen. Despite what was laughingly called training,

Charlie and I had no hope of ever getting our act together productively.

The antediluvian techno-god was an ugly great monster, occupying an entire wall of the small room called mine, and left no-one in any doubt as to who was really in charge.

A head would pop round the door from time to time to ask how I was getting on, making enthusiastic noises about the new technology in admiring tones, before disappearing with what seemed undue haste. By the end of my first week I began to suspect not one of them had a clue how to use it.

I suppose jobs could have been at risk if the bosses found out, so it was left to a naïve newcomer from the north to pretend she knew what she was doing.

I probably screwed poor Charlie up beyond all hope of recovery before I finally gave up and walked out. I would have been rumbled soon anyway, and almost certainly sacked.

What I thought I wanted to do was help people, so I applied to become a State Registered Nurse at St. George's hospital, back in west London where I felt much more at ease.

After a full day of mental and physical challenges, with a group of about fifteen other candidates all younger than me, I was surprised and delighted to be accepted for the course, despite the disastrous steady hand test. The 'got it wrong' bell rang every time I ran a hoop over a length of wire aiming to keep the two apart.

I could cope well enough with the ward routines, and loved the uniform, especially the scarlet-lined black cloak and distinctive head-dress, but one of the tutorial sisters clearly thought I was climbing the wrong mountain from the start, and made it her mission from day one to unsettle and if possible dislodge me.

Whenever an opportunity arose, Sister Parsons would fix me with a beady stare, causing me to shake while setting up a dressing trolley, or to flush crimson if asked a question in class.

With the hint of a sneer she pointed out that one of my shoe heels was worn down, and refused to accept cash for an expensive year two text book, eyeing me and my one pound notes with disdain. A fellow student wrote me a cheque.

After the patients had been settled down, and the kidney dishes and other steel equipment used through the day had been scrubbed and committed to the steriliser, I quite enjoyed night duty. Interesting things could happen then, like births and deaths, and car crash admissions, and somebody looking for their keys.

The scenario sometimes was positively surreal.

"Come to theatre quickly, Nurse. I need you to hold a patient's head."

I was alone in the rest room during the mid-shift break, listening to Frank Sinatra singing 'Fly me to the Moon'.

When a surgeon said jump, you jumped.

This was Wombles and anyone for tennis territory, but at two in the morning it could just as easily have been the brave new world or Timbuktu.

It was impossible to tell whether the life-form sitting bolt upright on a chair in the middle of otherwise empty space was male or female, dormant or awake, as only one small square of shaved scalp was visible. The two of us were dummies in alien terrain, equally unsure. The theatre was totally silent, until the drilling began.

At Hyde Park Corner you could watch gleaming dawn rays tiptoeing delicately across the waking city, and hear the clip-clop of early morning hooves on their way from the Knightsbridge barracks to Rotten Row.

With the gradually brightening sky car engines would rudely interrupt the dreaming, as busyness returned with bedside washes and cups of tea, and the day staff arriving.

Day or night made no difference to Ali. He was one of the first people in the country to be kept alive by modern technology. Health experts from far and wide came to stare at him with knowing nods, making copious notes.

Ali would almost certainly have icon status these days. His pallid shrinking figure was a fixture in the medical ward for years, with his cubicle curtains permanently drawn. New nurses were ushered behind them reverently for a viewing.

No-one knew who he was, where he came from, or what to do about him. One morning when we came on duty he was gone. Not one of us dared ask how why or where.

I was once given the responsibility of caring solo for a little boy called Nigel, who had a cancerous tumour in his brain at the age of four.

My faith in the goodness of the universe took quite a knock at the revelation that a small child could be so cruelly afflicted, but I loved looking after him, and couldn't wait for my shift to begin. When it ended I almost resented having to leave him in other hands.

When after three or four weeks his little life came to an end, the consultant took me aside to talk me through what had happened, and assure me I could have done nothing to save him.

I was deeply touched by the great man's concern. He asked me to write a case history for the hospital records describing Nigel's final weeks, as not much was known about the disease at the time. The task helped me a lot.

When the time came Matron let me go without much fuss. A married nurse by definition has divided loyalties, and although I had some of the qualities needed for the job she knew as well as I did that I had not found my true vocation.

In a department store environment once more, *the* department store no less, I had money to spend again and did so with glee, this time on household items for the long cardboard box under my bed, a space saving substitute for a bottom drawer in my very small room.

Harrods hire purchase department still sounds like a contradiction in terms to me, and it certainly did then. Credit was mostly frowned on at the time, very much so by my father. If you can't pay for it do without and save up was yesterday's ethic. We never told him about our first fridge.

An occasional lord of the realm or famous name on the books added a touch of glamour to the daily routine of servicing customer accounts and sending out late payment demands, but filing stuff no-one would ever look at again was a bit of a bore.

The lending library, free to staff, made daily strap-hanging a joy. Unwelcome interference by a predatory male was easily dealt with by a quick kick on the shin or stamp on a foot, accidentally on purpose, looking as if butter wouldn't melt. It invariably worked a treat. I even managed to fit in singing lessons again after work.

Although Harrods was a lovely place to be, my co-workers were great, and the Food Hall and Christmas Shop were nothing short of spectacular, I lived for mid-day on Saturday when Gloria arrived with her master, spruced up and ready to go.

***

The May bank holiday weekend that in 2016 began with John's eighty-third birthday, and ended with our fifty-seventh wedding anniversary, was a nightmare beyond imagination.

Transfer from wheelchair to sofa around ten the Thursday evening before had gone wrong, and after seven and a half years of single-handed caring I knew I was beaten.

The emergency services, as always, were insanely busy, so I made John as comfortable as I could on the floor, and just waited.

Next morning all hell was let loose. Bodies were vying for space, furniture and equipment was being moved or installed. An adjustable hospital bed arrived, and a scary-looking hoist.

Rapid response nurses were checking out the bathroom and medication, occupational therapists were making demands about seating arrangements and filling out forms.

John looked on silently from his wheelchair, only sketchily aware of what was going on. The fact that this actually was his birthday, the second since moving to the bungalow, was completely forgotten.

When the emergency team left around dawn we had slept in each other's arms, expecting to do the same until one or both of us ceased to be.

A few hours later we were zombies in the half light.

***

July/August 2017
Catch-Up

The power shower in our new home was impressive, with enough room for two. For a husband needing help it seemed perfect. For a wife with erratic bones however, liable to lose her balance at any moment without warning, it was an accident in waiting.

Before bed claimed him more or less permanently at the end of last May, John used to spend a lot of time trundling around the house in his wheelchair, following me from room to room when possible, exploring solo if not.

Whenever he heard the lively energy of water hitting the tiles, he would call out every few minutes to confirm I was still on my feet, telephone to hand just in case, hoping to give me a Swedish as soon as I reappeared on the scene.

He was a qualified masseur, and had sensitive hands, but simply could not understand why at times it was necessary to say no. A massage brought welcome relief when muscle tension was the only problem, but if overstretch and edgy nerves were involved it could make things worse.

He decided to check out the shower for himself one day, while I was busy with domestic chores. By the time I became aware of what was happening he was hanging on by his finger-tips to the metal-framed door precariously poised, with his arms turning shades of purplish blue. Leaving him alone to find a phone was absolutely not an option.

I spent the rest of the morning pulling at his clothing, and nudging his body and feet this way and that, to ease him inch by inch back into his wheelchair. Moribund muscle tissue was robbing him daily of the ability to move, so despite visible weight loss he felt incredibly heavy.

My own muscles are still quite painful at times, as they strive to accommodate the demands of a relatively new, perfectly aligned hip. Moving an arm can cause overstretch in a hip or leg, and a body turn sometimes cramps muscles quite seriously in the chest and abdomen.

Good pain, the post-op physios called it as they waved me cheerfully on my way, nothing to worry about, part of getting better not worse. They omitted to mention that every bit of me might need time to adjust, that pain could keep resurfacing somewhere in my body for years.

That apart, with the nagging hollow stomach syndrome now becoming a rarity I am eating more sensibly, sleeping better, and beginning to feel much more myself.

I even renewed my passport recently ready to expand horizons next year, and two decades after qualifying for one finally possess a bus pass.

With the luxury of a bath and me-friendly shower, my long-jaded nerves are at last fairly docile. Bubble-soak, Classic FM, no clock equals bliss.

I have everything I need, except the love of my life.

***

John and I were married in a Methodist chapel on a traffic jammed road in Hounslow, with a lacy white dress and flimsy veil. Shoppers stopped by briefly to wish us well then headed for Woolworths.

My two bridesmaids came to see us off at Heathrow, in peaches and cream wedding attire with matching head-dress and white satin shoes. It was very exciting.

On reflection I suppose church was hypocritical, but despite no longer believing it seemed like the right thing to do, and kept my parents happy, especially Mum.

With me off their hands they moved to a bungalow in Bognor, hoping the sea air might help to improve her health. She was painfully thin.

With cancer already embarked on its unrelenting march, they probably knew before moving that their days together were coming to a premature end, but at least there was a proper garden to sit out in again, and plenty of space for an easel.

We used to go to Morecambe sometimes when I was small. The seaweed in the bay was supposed to be beneficial for chesty conditions. More often than not it made things worse.

"Mummy's not very well this morning darling," Daddy would say, after one or two days at the boarding house. "We can build sand castles if you like, and sail your yacht on the pond. Mummy may be ready to come out later, when she's had a good rest."

She never was. The two of us walked the length of the promenade to Heysham quite often without her, and played for pennies in the amusement arcade when it rained. As soon as the local doctor said she was well enough to travel, we collected our ration books from the landlady and took the train home.

In retrospect rationing was not all bad, in some ways socially good. At a time when snacks and fizzy drinks were reserved for the occasional treat obesity was uncommon, in children practically non-existent.

The planet had a better deal back then too. Sturdy shopping bags could be reused for years, and water came free from a tap, with not a scrap of plastic waste.

I gave up on religion when I was seventeen, after attending an evangelical gig at a sports arena in north London. The celebrity preacher from across the pond had an impressive physique with ego to match, and a voice that could melt ice cold steel. He was almost as charismatic as Elvis, and for some people just as hard to resist.

"We are all miserable sinners," he boomed through the microphone in doom-laden tones, "headed for an ugly unpleasant and unending end if we don't mend our ways very soon." Little Miss Marshall meek and mild this most certainly was not.

When the proclamations of hell and damnation and assurances that God could cure all ills were over crowds flocked mindlessly onto the pitch, to make a pledge most would regret by tomorrow. Feeling unaccountably sad, I made straight for the exit and the nearest underground station.

I suppose I went there looking for a lifeline. My years of attending Sunday school had done little to convince me, but some of the Bible stories made me feel good inside, and a comfort blanket can be very hard to let go.

In my quiet moments though I realised a God who cared for each of us individually was for me a fantasy too far. Evidence to the contrary seemed to be everywhere around us. It is even more so now.

Rome has always scared me stiff, with its 'see you next week Jack' confessionals, reputation for sexual misconduct, and sometimes inhuman doctrines. Was contraception really so wrong in an overpopulated world peppered with sex-obsessed men? Was poor little Nigel a sinner?

Clever men with creative imaginations messed our heads up for all time when they invented religion.

Even the transparently fictional Greek gods seemed somehow more acceptable, having the honesty to get on with adultery and whatever other vices took their fancy without apology or remorse. They hardly bothered at all about their puny little earthlings, and left them to flounder in self-created chaos as a matter of course.

I doubt John ever believed. Bullying and injustices at school in Scotland, where he was sent at the age of eight to keep him safe from the war, had made him a sceptic for life.

He loved the forest where he lived, and the anthills and the bees, but dreaded school like living hell. Due to the unfamiliar accent he was unable to stand up for himself against the lies of his scheming contemporaries, and was easily set up. His creature-kindly hands were meanly abused daily for crimes other boys committed.

Back at home he was a stranger all over again, with a lot of catching up to do. Most of his southern class mates had stayed put through the war, with no interruption to their schooling. He never forgave his parents for sending him away.

John's own family though meant absolutely everything to him. The four of us made up a perfect nuclear unit, with a boy arriving first, girl second, just as we had hoped.

When they were babies he made them laugh before settling them down to sleep each night, sometimes causing hiccups, and played football and snakes and ladders with them for years.

The bones parade already sowing seeds of future havoc in my body had ensured neither birth was easy (one forceps, one induced three weeks late) but the end result was just as it should be.

My father's irrational bouts of fury, and tendency to bend the truth about his professional qualifications had troubled me for years, but only after Mum died did I seriously begin to question his state of mind.

He kept her body in their bedroom for a week, in a coffin lined with pink satin, holding a posy of mixed flowers. The house reeked of death.

"Have you visited Mummy yet, darling?" he would ask every day, with an ominous air of calm. I lived in dread of what might follow.

The subtle changes in his all too mortal masterpiece seemed to escape him entirely, even when her poor little mouth began to fall open, and the flowers fell drooping from her hands.

As soon as I began to show an interest in adult affairs, Dad used to apply a tourniquet to my curiosity on the pretext that I was too young to understand, so I learned early to keep my thoughts to myself.

In truth I probably knew more about real life than he did. When just once I asked his advice from grown-up to grown-up he said I was old enough to sort out my own problems. I wasn't, but then neither was he. At that moment a door closed inside me. It never quite opened again.

In the early days of marriage John would put a damper on my long ingrained habit of reading. From one controlling male to another I thought, simmering inside.

So when I started studying again some years later his change of attitude was an agreeable surprise. He even built a special purpose unit in our bedroom, with a bench and plenty of book space, where I could escape to read and write whenever I liked.

Other men seemed to find their place in the scheme of things threatened by a wife's educational aspirations, but mine gave me limitless support.

I thoroughly enjoyed university, although my approach to critical analysis was not disciplined enough for some of the lecturers, many of whom seemed to like my way with words, but not always the logic.

My reading of D. H. Lawrence on religion was so wrong that I managed to reverse what was actually being said, but then he was a confused rebel too.

With a mountain of real books to get through, and a family and house to look after, time was at a premium, so believing I should be formulating my own views not reflecting theirs I ignored the literary critics, despite being asked for knowledgeable quotes to bump up marks in the Finals.

Just once I scored an academic bull's eye, well almost. As the professor handed back my essay on Wordsworth and Shelley with the single word yes, my heart leapt with joy.

After a moment's pause though she added, "I'm not sure about—"

I don't remember the precise adverb in question, possibly or probably perhaps or maybe, even very. I knew exactly where it was on the page. It had been in and out of the essay many times.

John loved a good wrestling match, both physical and mental, and had found his young wife's lack of enthusiasm for either disappointing. Discovering he had married a child, with a woman inside fearful to come out, his aim from the start was to grow her.

I graduated at the age of forty, good in parts.

***

At the beginning of July last year the thermometer said John's temperature was normal, but he had choked quite dramatically on a spoonful of breakfast cereal that morning.

The emergency services talked me through what to do on the phone until someone came to help, by which time he had recovered, or so I thought.

"Choking is not a good way to go, better to sort it out now," said the district nurse facing me sorrowfully across the kitchen table. "We can look after him here, if that's what he wants."

Look after that time felt suspiciously like a euphemism. I had expected a routine check. Was she really suggesting what I thought she was suggesting?

John was adamant that he wanted to stay at home, and refused point blank to sign the 'Do Not Resuscitate' form.

"Not yet," he said, with the wild look of a cornered animal. He did not believe he was at the point of no return.

In my heart, neither did I.

He was not capable of signing, so the dreadful task would fall to me. I felt very afraid.

"How long will it take?" I asked helplessly, squeezing the question out through a chattering jaw.

"Three to five days."

My head began to reel, and I had to sit down. I had hoped for at least six more weeks.

Only the day before we had cried together, just a little, for what had been and what inevitably was to come. Then my dear love's face suddenly cleared, he said he felt better, and what had happened to the promised strawberries and cream.

Neither of us was ready yet for the final goodbye. Were we really going to just let him die?

As he grew steadily more feverish through a very long night I soothed his forehead with damp cotton wool, and moistened his lips with cool water. By morning my heart felt like lead.

To my relief, the doctor who came to authorise the fateful 'pathway' punched the facts straight at us, with no suspicion of a deflecting velvet glove.

John had aspirant pneumonia. Food that should be going into his stomach was getting into his lungs. He needed urgent treatment. Did he want to go into hospital or stay at home?

Same question, different answer.

An ambulance arrived within the hour.

***

September/October 2017
Changing Times

My intrepid dreamer spent most of last year's July in hospital, on a sieved food and thickened liquids diet he absolutely hated.

From the moment the pneumonia subsided, and he was able to tolerate the real thing again, he pestered everyone from cleaner to consultant relentlessly about coming home. His bleak glassy eyes broke my heart as they followed me to the end of the ward each afternoon, terrified it might never happen.

Back in his own room, with nursing care four times a day, me on twenty-four hour call, a spoonful of chopped bacon with egg for breakfast, and his children dropping by when they could, he was quietly content.

I kept the pressure mattress switched on 24/7 while he was away, so as not to tempt fate. Although he would never leave his bed again, it was wonderful to have him home.

The Parkinson's medication had been cancelled, and hallucinations were a thing of the past.

I sat with him in the afternoons, sometimes talking, sometimes not. Occasionally I would read to him from my latest writings. He seemed to enjoy this, especially the bits about Gloria getting stuck, and 'Hey Little Hen'.

"The book is about us," I told him. "You are the most important character. If I get it right, you will be famous."

The purr inside showed briefly on his face.

He had been trying for some time to write down what Parkinson's was doing to him, to benefit other sufferers after he was gone, but when his mind grew lazy, and his writing became illegible, he had to give in.

We had tried dictation earlier in the year, but he usually fell asleep before I picked up a pen.

***

Engineering is not my natural environment, yet when an editorial post became available at John's place of work they offered me the job. I had to sign the official secrets act, and was asked if I would be comfortable working on government assignments.

I had already been living off them for twenty years, so this was hardly the moment to retreat to already compromised moral high ground. When it came to it the content of most of the documents I had to deal with meant little to me anyway, and I still know nothing about John's work, except that printed circuit boards were involved.

He had hoped I would be employed in HR (what used to be Personnel) when he showed me the advert in the staff magazine, dealing with people not national security, but to protect domestic confidentiality that was not permitted. The technical post I was offered turned out to be a perfect fit.

The section was in total disarray when I arrived. My predecessor was approaching retirement, ready and eager to initiate the wind down. Faced with the prospect of a cyber-driven future he was utterly lost. Being side-lined to tidy up old files suited him just fine.

Frazzled typists at the point of mutiny were relieved to be told what to do by someone with two feet in the present and at least one eye on the future.

While management groups were preparing to implement new techniques, they and I carried on with the old ones. In an age where cut and paste involved scissors and glue, and diagrams were created with a ruler and pencil, I was totally in my element.

We once worked through the night to meet the deadline for an important presentation, beginning a fourteen hour stint as lone operators, and heading for breakfast next morning as a team.

When strategies and policies, hardware and software, and who should collect the coffees had been agreed, we were sent to London for a day to learn about word processing and computer basics, and to get a feel for the paperless society everyone was raving about at the time.

Lunch at a nearby pizza restaurant, with as much salad as you liked and a free glass of wine, was a revelation.

Mediterranean cuisine had yet to reach the Berkshire Oxfordshire border. The moment it did John created what would remain his signature dish for the rest of his life.

We ate Anglo-Italian bolognese with unmanageably long spaghetti for the best part of four decades, which seemed exotic at first, especially with Chianti in a peasant-style raffia holder, but I'm still on the fence about garlic.

John's cooking repertoire expanded through ensuing years, to include home-grown vegetables, hand-baked bread, home-made soup, and Chateau Ratsey wine, but rarely puddings.

Almost imperceptibly the man of the house evolved into head chef, apologising at first for taking over *my* kitchen.

Like I minded! Most of the time I actually preferred crackers and cheese and washing-up.

Some aspects of equality have always seemed questionable to me, risking everyone losing out in the end, especially the children. But with mine almost grown up, and female equanimity unsettled for all time by the militant feminists of the day, once the new system at work was properly established I began to feel restless, or as if I ought to feel restless. There was nothing new for me to do, and people with my mix of recently acquired skills were in high demand.

John considered it brave but foolish to apply for a job at the very heart of the rapidly advancing digital scene. He hated the new-fangled CAD (Computer Aided Design) currently displacing his trusty drawing board and T-Square, and feared we were rushing blindly towards a world of acronyms and sound bites where trivia was king, and meaningful communication would be relegated bit by byte to the do not recycle bin.

American companies demanded your soul, and all your waking hours, or so he believed. We argued about it a lot.

I became moody, and took to taking long solo walks, and holding earnest conversations with next door's tortoise. Yet again I was being held back from being me, or at least from the kind of me I thought I wanted to be. What was it about men?

The generous salary, monthly trips to Geneva and twice a year to the States seemed very attractive to me, but alcohol laced evenings in glamorous locations were uppermost in my husband's ever watchful mind. He knew about men.

Observing the experiences of some of his peers at the time, he was probably not too sure about women either. Given the freedom of the pill, even those who should have known better were treating sex as a game. Marriages that should have stayed solid as a rock were being devalued daily, for the sake of an experimental fling.

When a typist offered me a room for as long as I might need to sort myself out I was tempted, but after a spot of soul-searching realised that if I walked there would be no way back, and John might never recover.

"We have seen several candidates for this position already," the Chief Editor told me, an hour and a half into the interview in his paper-piled office on a very hot afternoon. "None of them came close to speaking editing language, but now you are here."

He sounded like the cat that got the cream, and handed over a hefty technical manual in the manner of an admirer bestowing a priceless gift.

"You'll make light work of this, I'm sure."

The error-strewn document was to be returned by the following Monday, marked up ready for correction.

We were going on holiday the next day.

"Oh, and we shall need a full description of how to make a cup of tea for someone who has never done it before," he added, as I was about to leave.

A cup of tea!

I spent most of the evening with an A4 pad and pen, detailing every nuance of the mundane task from 'Turn on the tap, half fill a kettle with cold water and bring it to the boil' to 'finally add milk and sugar to taste, stir with a teaspoon, and enjoy'.

Disapproving eyes boring the words 'what did I tell you' into the back of my head made it hard to concentrate, but the packing would just have to wait.

Why full English was needed was far from clear. With the exception of terms and conditions in miniscule print the trend ever since has been towards linguistic minimalism, along the lines of 1.Place tea-bag in cup, 2.Turn on tap etc.

Perhaps I misunderstood.

The manual came with us to Cornwall. John was incensed.

The week was decidedly wet. While he and the children played Scrabble and Canasta on the floor, and took soggy walks to the site shop over rain-washed sands, I sat at a table in a corner of the caravan scribbling furiously for our supper.

Back home on the job, fault lines began to appear very soon. With every passing day I became more and more withdrawn, less and less able to think.

Colleagues seemed constantly on edge, and kept looking around furtively to check if anyone had overheard my latest controversial remark.

With the technological revolution advancing apace, everyone was keen to prove their worth. Fear of making even the smallest mistake hung in the air like a mischievous troll. Before long I started looking over my shoulder too.

One word one meaning was anathema to someone who had immersed herself in the between lines subtleties of the English language for most of her first forty years. I made an appointment to see the big boss.

Contrary to my overblown imaginings, Big Brother was a mild mannered man, so far as I could tell entirely devoid of any soul snatching aspirations. As well as a string of technical qualifications old and new he had a doctorate in psychology, and a wonderfully reassuring Yorkshire accent.

There was no clock in the room, yet not once did he glance at his watch. By the time we were through, he knew me better than I knew myself.

"You need to decide what matters most in your life," he advised. "Go home now. We'll send your money on."

The three month trial contract I had put my name to with pride and defiance was not even mentioned.

"When you have made up your mind, let me know whether or not you wish to come back."

Two days later I wrote to thank him for his kindness.

Assistant Editor of the in-house magazine for the local John Lewis felt more like a hobby than work. Part-time low tech, spiked with a weekly confrontation with she who must be obeyed, set me wonderfully free.

The Editor was the branch registrar, who had the final say on what could and could not be published. My article about the icicle cluster flamboyantly encircling a drain pipe outside a second floor window was thrown out on the spot, which seemed a pity.

The girls in the fashion alterations room had been looking forward to getting a mention in the magazine for once, and the photos were really rather good. I cut a finger and laddered my tights leaning out of a window. I don't suppose that was allowed either.

Dear Dorothea invariably found it more important to drool over someone's new baby, or drink tea with the managing director, than to provide information I needed to do my job within a usually squeezed timeline. It's fair to say there was a personality clash right from the start.

"Eether, dear," she corrected me at our first weekly policy meeting, "not eyether. Neether, not nyether."

As far as I was concerned this was not negotiable. I simply ignored her.

The ageing typewriters and five foot long collating machine created their own mini dramas by going on strike from time to time, holding up copy and pushing deadlines, but that just added to the fun. Once again I had a great little team.

Most important of all, with the domestic boat back on an even keel my shining knight was carefree and happy again, and suggested we should join a dance school.

He had attended a few classes in his youth, and knew enough to guide me round the floor and make up steps for holidays and Christmas, but it had never occurred to either of us to take up dancing seriously.

I gave us six months max.

***

The studiously avoided topic came up the moment I entered the room.

"I don't like you having to do this on your own."

I drew a sharp breath. The experts were urging me yet again to think of myself. They simply did not understand. This was John's time. All I had to do was survive.

But much had changed since making the original decision. Suppose I was getting it wrong.

Was he hankering for something different, more people perhaps, was he fed up with me? There was only one way to find out.

"Would you rather be in a care home, with a team of people to look after you?" I asked tentatively, fighting hard to suppress a surge of rising panic.

He tried with all his might to heave his totally immobile back from the bed, mustering every scrap of energy to shout "No!" Tears poured in rivulets down his cheeks.

"That's all I need to know, my love, that truly is all I need to know."

I hugged him as best I could, and my tears mingled softly with his.

***

November 2017
Turmoil

21B was tucked away in a dingy block behind the main shopping street in Reading, with no windows and poor lighting.

The tiny reception area was functional (just about) with a few chairs and coat hooks, and a huge pile of vinyl LP's.

The only touch of glitz was a mirrored wall at the far end of the dance-floor that gave an illusion of space and twice as many people. By the time the introductory course ended we were hooked.

"I don't usually do private lessons for beginners," said Ben, trying not to sound too pompous (we were paying customers after all). "Nothing less than gold medal level as a rule."

Noting our blank faces, after a brief pause he continued, "Will Saturday mornings suit?"

He partnered me himself occasionally, to find out what I could do, sometimes a lot, sometimes a flop. Spins along a straight line came easily to most ladies, even those who barely knew their right foot from their left. I shot off at a tangent every single time.

Ben was clearly puzzled. So was I.

"I like your left leg," he said, observing every move of our foxtrot intently.

"What's wrong with the right one?" I retaliated, not really expecting an answer.

My hips apparently turned the wrong way too.

Personally, I was amazed they turned at all. So far as I was aware they never had before.

Toy boys were a hot topic at the time, and everyone at the school decided it was the teacher I was obsessed with not the dancing, but they were wrong. Ben taught me things about my body that I might never have known, but John was always and ever my one and only.

We danced several times a week, wherever they played the right music, cementing ever more surely our unique brand of togetherness. The headaches that had plagued me from my teens miraculously vanished.

As weeks stretched to months and months to years we grew ever closer. You can be as one on a dance-floor for hours at a time without speaking a word.

Then sciatica struck like a flash of lightning, and joints everywhere in my body vied feverishly for the right to attack me. Chiropractic took over our lives, with treatments every day to start with, spacing out over time.

"Keep going," 'they' said, "keep working, keep dancing. Activity seems to suit you."

"I don't play at dancing," I said loftily, as if I knew everything there was to know on the subject after a mere five years practice. "I try to do the footwork correctly – heel to toe ballroom, ball-flat Latin, straighten your legs and don't look at the floor, that sort of stuff."

"Good for you," they said, unsurprisingly not impressed.

The trouble was I over-practised and over-analysed technique, and agonised about dancing in general. Other people just did it and enjoyed.

My body really did not like me. I paced the living room eating meals, knelt on a cushion at the office to type, and slept on the floor at the foot of our bed, taking up to two hours to ease out screeching joints in order to get to my feet each morning.

Walking upstairs was good, coming down a disaster. One day I found myself lying in the gutter outside the British Home Stores after getting off a bus. The faces looking down at me plainly thought I was drunk, or on a high.

Standard pain killers did not work, but having no wish to court morphine addiction I decided not to make a fuss. The only thing that provided temporary relief was dancing.

The John Lewis physiotherapist understood better than I did what was going on in my body, yet she too was puzzled.

"Your posture is better than mine," she said, "but something somewhere isn't right."

She tried mimicking what seemed to be wrong by moving her own feet and hips. "You must have done something like this."

Before my very eyes she performed a perfect rumba-style figure of eight. I was seriously impressed.

It seemed to me we were being side-lined at the dance school, so initially almost for fun I became mildly disruptive, ensuring we arrived late for classes to miss the partner-changing warm-up, pacing the dance-floor in meditative silence during the coffee break, and similar antics.

This did not go down well, but there was a genuine reason for my deliberately anti-social behaviour. In my highly sensitive physical state, having started moving it was imperative to keep going to prevent joints from seizing up, and only John or Ben could be relied on as partners. This was difficult to explain without causing offence or seeming to seek preference.

Hysterical tears in the car park were not unusual at the end of a class, giving rise to even more speculation about my emotional involvement with Ben.

"You'd shoot a horse in this condition," I ventured, during the essential late night walk needed to soothe my seething body.

John could only agree.

Then as suddenly as it came the sciatic electric current switched off, which meant at least one less problem to deal with. I was briefly euphoric, but worse was to come.

When a vertebra slipped out of true with a quietly ominous pop I could not lie down at all, or pick up a loaf of bread. Inflamed tendons raged like a burning fire at the base of my spine.

I spent the nights taking cat-naps in a chair, in between pacing the sitting room and doing the ironing, washing an already clean kitchen floor, or mopping non-existent cobwebs from the ceiling. There was a movement somewhere that could put everything right, I felt sure.

The car was torture, buses not much better. At times I could not bear to be touched. I walked where I could, but finally could do nothing at all, and apart from chiropractic visits found myself grounded for months, wondering if the nightmare would ever end.

My body and I were at war, scarily disconnected. A glance in the mirror showed a Notre Dame hunchback with a protruding breast-bone, the top of the right leg slightly overlapping the left, and a half-closed left eye.

As things very slowly started to improve, and body and soul began tenuously talking to one another again, I plucked up courage to try lying on the bed.

As I stretched inch by inch from top to toe and extended both arms sideways, my ribcage cracked noisily back into place giving me a fright, but nothing bad followed.

Then just as I was thinking maybe it was safe to begin easing life back towards some kind of normality, my reliably unreliable hormones took centre stage for one final fling.

John drove me straight to A & E, where I suppose I must have passed out. I woke up during the visiting hour attached to a drip, aware of people conversing in hushed tones at the next bed.

"My aunt was like that. She was only fifty-one. Fit as a fiddle on Saturday. Admitted on Sunday. By Wednesday she was dead."

Solomon Grundy. Was this still Sunday? My mum was fifty-one.

With other people's blood pouring straight through me, and the grim reaper almost certainly on his way, I felt curiously calm. The only thought in my otherwise empty head was it would have been nice to dance a good paso doble.

Seven pints and two tumultuous days and nights later my body began to respond, and quite soon I felt fine.

I was back home by Wednesday, more relaxed than I had been in a long time.

As if by magic sex improved, with a nod at last towards the full Monty. Though still not perfect, the improved connection made us both very happy.

***

When the carers arrived John was just finishing off his breakfast yoghurt. I picked up the tray ready to leave, anxious not to get in their way.

"How are you today?" Bernie asked.

He was a salt of the earth Geordie, compassionate to the core, and had recently travelled to India to marry his girlfriend in her home village. Soon he would be going off again, this time locally, to train as a plumber. We would miss him.

He placed a soft ball in John's screwed up hand, to stop his own nails from digging holes in the palm.

For the first time in a week I was not wearing a handkerchief over my nose and mouth to protect our patient from a persistent cold.

I was feeling much better that morning, and said so.

A voice piped up cheerfully from the bed.

"The corpse is all right too."

A wry smile with the merest hint of a twinkle momentarily rolled back years.

When Bernie and Lyn had gone John seemed anxious, so I cradled his delicate pale hands in mine and waited.

"I didn't trust you enough," he said at last, seeking my eyes like a lost child through a misted windscreen.

Did he mean now, or ever?

"I need to rethink my attitude about you," he went on.

From the day we first met, or in the present situation?

I assured him he had done and was doing brilliantly, that everything between us was just fine. Then I kissed his lips lightly, and began moving towards the kitchen.

"I'll go make some tea."

A plaintive voice called after me, "Pam-ella."

The recently adopted musical version of my name made me smile. I turned back.

"Everybody's written me off, haven't they – the nurses, doctors, everybody?"

I pretended not to hear.

"All they have to offer is palliative drivel."

At least his vocabulary was still intact. We had 'alacrity' and 'discombobulated' the other day.

After a long drawn out pause he added, "Don't forget to thank them, will you?"

***

December 2017
Joined-Up Writing

In mid-October thirty years ago, the country awoke to media reports of fallen trees, and extensive damage to property in several counties. On the same date this year the news was much the same, although the damage this time was much less severe.

On the evening of what would later be dubbed the storm of the twentieth century John and I were at the Albert Hall, enjoying the finals of an international dance competition with a group of pupils from a friend's classes.

Emma had left Ben's school some time before to teach independently, and since making the decision to do the same ourselves we had been helping her out, useful for her, good experience for us.

We spent the evening in a red and gold second floor box, with smoked salmon and champagne. A plaque near the door reminded us in elegant script to arrange 'Carriages at Midnight'.

In the interval we all went down to dance on the celebrated floor, unaware that nature was busily making mischief outside our glamorously whirling bubble.

Our minibus was buffeted by side winds on the M4, causing treacherous sway, but with adrenaline levels high and voices in competitive free flow none of us paid much attention.

John and I stayed the night with Emma and her non-dancing husband Michael, in their rambling old house in Hampshire with window seats and an overgrown paddock, not far from the spot where Gloria gave her diva display on a notable night in our past.

We chatted idly about dancing and golf, and of life's little quirks, warmed by spicy fruit punch and a roaring log fire, with flickering flames dancing lightly on the ceiling.

Shortly before dawn, all talked out and woozy, we climbed the stairs with candles and bed socks, and slept like babes until late the next morning.

We are only one now.

***

By October last year we knew our days were numbered. Loose ends practical and emotional had all been dealt with, and as far as the situation allowed we were content just to be.

My steadily declining love became extremely agitated a few days before he died. There was something he absolutely had to get off his chest.

We had just finished our evening meal, using one dish two spoons, one for him, one for me. Not that either of us ate much, but we both played the game.

Into the companionable silence John suddenly shouted "Go!" with extraordinary passion. "Go now," he commanded, staring intently into my eyes. "What are you waiting for? Get out onto the stage. Go!"

His body was more alive than it had been in months, and his voice was firm and strong. If I moved towards him even slightly every bit of him seemed to say don't touch, you need to listen, this is about you, not about me. So I stood still and waited.

After a moment's pause he started bossing me about again, with undiminished fervour. "Go now! Take a bow. Your audience is waiting. You must not disappoint."

***

John's funeral took place in the conservatory on a sunny December day. His willow-green casket sparkled with bright flowers.

Family and neighbours came, and friends old and new. The words spoken were simple and true.

He lies at peace now in a green wooded glade caressed by rain wind and sun, forever at one with the nature he loved.

The white-beam tree planted for him a few months ago is coming along nicely. With winter settling in its leaves are mostly fallen. When fate decrees, I shall join him in its shade.

***

While preparing for the house move three years ago I came across 'The Return of Cupid', dated 1940, amongst other of Dad's paintings out of sight and mind for years.

As I cleared the grime of ages from the protective glass, the back board fell out, to reveal a second painting dated 1934, of my parents looking down lovingly at a baby boy crawling near them on the floor.

I knew at once that this was my longed for older brother, that Cupid had come to take one child away, and deliver another.

A teddy bear was sitting nearby, and a black boy doll with tight curly hair and a smiley face. He was wearing a bright red blazer with shiny gold buttons, and blue and white check trousers like Mrs. Rabbity's pinafore. I remembered playing with him in the far distant past, before political correctness was invented. His name was Sam.

Both paintings hang on my bedroom wall today, minus the cobwebs exactly as I found them. The narrow black frame now makes sense.

The flimsily draped lady with sad eyes went straight to landfill. We had gone our separate ways during intervening years, and the blatantly untrue art qualification appended to her canvas since our last encounter hurt my soul. The word 'Loveless' was pencilled on the back. I had never noticed it before.

The flashy engagement ring shown to me with pride within weeks of Mum's demise went into the waste bin too. It might have been valuable, could equally have been trash. The new love might or might not have existed. I really did not care.

The sliver of hatred that scarred my heart, at a time when I was still devastated by my own recent loss, may never truly heal.

Only when both painting and ring were gone did I see that the desperate lies were Dad's way of letting me know things were going to be all right, when as time later proved they patently were not. He too was a smoker.

Recognising the complexities of truth too late, I screamed in frustrated fury at a deity I had long ceased to believe in.

***

I started playing the piano again recently, or tried to. Even after a very long gap my head seems to know what to do well enough, but persuading all ten fingers to respond with the confidence and accuracy of the past is an uphill task.

I have known from early teens that my hands are out of sync, with the left fingers striking the notes fractionally ahead of the right, a failing no amount of practice can overcome. My teacher knew something was wrong way back then. At the time I thought nothing of it, but things are different now.

The wider implications of one arm being set slightly further back than the other have become graphically apparent of late.

At last I can see how the ill-fitting bras, disappearing left sock and rubbing shoe, not to mention a whole range of other mysterious aberrations, have played their part in the history of my chronically capricious bones.

Every bit of my body has been affected through the years, from top of head to big toe. Several organs have raised false alarms needing various health tests, including ECG, and even an on the spot internal biopsy (horribly painful without anaesthetic, but over in a flash). Stuck tissues straining for freedom have intermittently caused unexplained bruises at numerous body sites in the past, and occasionally still do.

Crossed pelvic bones made sitting still for any length of time excruciating for years, and caused two spectacular falls doing Viennese turns, practically knocking me out on the dance-floor. John managed to protect my head the first time we went down, the second not quite.

Love in our two sets of misaligned bones was never going to be perfect. Ultimately we both understood. Neither of us was to blame. I was rigid, not frigid. John was just a bit skewed.

A partnership between Capricorn white rose and Gemini red is not supposed to work, but in our case two wrongs made a right. If John's parents had not moved to London from Liverpool before he was born, he and I would never even have met.

***

A young EU carer poured out her heart to me one day while filling the bowl for John's morning wash. "It must be wonderful to have one special person who will always love you no matter what."

Her longing expressed the emptiness of an era where trial before commitment is the norm, and saying no to sex before marriage is out of fashion.

The irony is that in a society where boundaries are almost non-existent, and credit gives us everything right now, fewer people than ever before seem to be truly happy.

***

As winter's pale rays tiptoed across my pillow this morning I dreamed a strange dream. People were preparing food in what felt but did not look like my kitchen. I had no idea what was in the cupboards or how to use the oven, where the kettle was, or how to turn on a light. As nobody seemed to notice me I wandered off in the gathering gloom.

The house was big, with large rooms and small rooms and corridors between, but no doors and no stairs. There was a nursery, a music room, and garden shed – a sweet shop, wine store and spa. In the distance church bells were ringing out for Christmas.

The further I roamed the more rooms I found, with walls now hewn out of rock, mostly with people, one, two, or many, eating and drinking, leaping or sleeping. A wistful young man with a musical voice was reading lines from Shelley (Percy Bysshe to his friends).

"And the sunlight clasps the earth, And the moonbeams kiss the sea, What are all these kissings worth, If thou kiss not me?"

In one room there was just an empty chair.

A steam train trundled by with no rails, blowing its whistle with a note of shrill defiance.

Before disappearing round the corner in a puff of smoke the driver called back, "The next will be the last, you must not miss it. The next *will* be the last."

Then the scene opened out, and I found myself in an enormous arena, a kind of Cheddar Gorge with tiers of seats from floor to ceiling, and people talking, industrially talking.

When a spotlight came on, shining directly at me, the arena fell silent. Every head turned as one to fix a thousand eyes upon me, and the babble instantly ceased, as if someone had pulled a string or flipped a switch.

A rippling sound emanating from the earth's core spread gradually from bottom to top of the cavernous chamber, until the walls seemed ready to split their sides with cacophonous laughter.

I looked down to find I was wearing a long flowing gown and high heels, holding a cricket bat in my hand.

Someone threw a ball, and I hit it for six.

***

Although dancing undoubtedly triggered my long latent back problems, it was in no way to blame for the mayhem that followed, and comes highly recommended. Both our teachers were first class.

The posture-friendly techniques of Strictly-style basics can sometimes help to sort out back problems, so after traction and manipulation had done what they could we moved to a different school to take teaching exams, then went off to find pupils of our own.

Few people who came to us would ever have dreamed of joining a dance school, but many stayed for years. Dancing is a wonderful way to escape from reality.

One young couple had an infant with cerebral palsy needing constant attention. They always looked drained when they arrived for a class, but invariably walked away with a smile.

A spinster in her sixties had been sole carer for an ailing mother for more than twenty years. She was very hard to move, and I say that with feeling. One of the disadvantages of being a woman dance teacher is you must also be willing and able to dance as man, smiling whatever the load.

I was most shocked of all to discover that the child of one of my long-term private couples had been murdered years before, on a stretch of heathland where the children and I used to pick blackberries.

***

Failing to find an exercise class to their liking, some pupils suggested I should start one of my own. So I did.

When reports began coming in about relief from aches and pains we realised our pesky bones could possibly be put to good social use, and became quite excited.

John did everything he could to help by taking videos, checking out moves, and most of all by criticising. He was sometimes rather too good at that, but not a word went to waste.

My ever faithful hero supported me for as long as he possibly could, even in his wheelchair, but fate had other plans.

***

Shortly after our fifteen minutes of exhilarating connection on a Henley dance-floor my spine slipped its moorings again, and chiropractic came back into our lives.

Once more my back very gradually improved, and we continued to teach, but by March 2012 a badly damaged hip could no longer be ignored.

The attentive young nurse from warmer climes ushered me into the lift with disbelieving awe, as if my determined limping gait and untroubled heart rate indicated a hide clad creature from another planet, rather than a mere human being about to undergo surgery.

"Are you nervous?" she asked, not for the first time, seeming a little anxious herself. She was probably new.

The pain that had punctuated my life for decades would soon be a thing of the past. The niggling whys and wherefores cluttering my chronically tormented brain were about to be resolved. My nerves were as quiet as I could ever remember.

Stick in hand I stepped a little too jauntily out of the lift, veering into a wall. A steadying arm set me straight.

In my day patients were wheeled to theatre on a trolley, in the rose-tinted fuzz of a pre-med. Things had changed.

Decades too late for poor Andy though. After being kept in bed for a week after his op, he dropped dead the moment his feet touched the floor. He had so looked forward to paddling in the sea with his small granddaughter.

"Why Tutu?" I asked, to fill an awkward silence.

"That was my Gran when I was four. She met the archbishop on a visit to Cape Town, and thought I would make a lovely dancer."

Her reminiscent giggle was a joy.

"Can you honestly imagine me tripping the light fantastic on my toes in a frilly frock?"

Without losing a kilo or two first I could not.

In the theatre I was greeted by a petite pretty nurse wearing slacks and a t-shirt, and a six foot male anaesthetist sporting heavily tattooed arms.

T-shirts used only to be worn in the gym or for sport, and trousers were for factory and farm girls, and men.

The tattooed lady was a freak in a fairground side show, next to the gypsy in a tent with crystal ball.

Things surely had changed.

"The long and the short of it," I quipped with a smile, as a needle slipped into my spine, and a gas mask was presented to my face.

Five and three-quarter years on my wayward bones are finally back where they should have remained all along, almost.

***

On a magical night in July I walked barefoot in the moonlit garden. The grass between my toes was cool and damp. Scents of summer floated lightly on the soft warm air.

I stood under the old apple tree, at one with the vastness of the sky, losing myself in the look of love that had remained unchanged through six decades.

The voice that had always sustained me filled my head and thrilled my heart.

"It's nice here, isn't it?"

It is.

***